Psychological Ramblings

Of A Traveling Gypsy

A definitive guide to Feminine Mystique, Power & Seduction

KAREMA MCGHEE

First published by Luxinous 2021

Copyright © 2021 by Karema McGhee

All rights reserved. No part of this publication may be reproduced, stored or transmitted in any form or by any means, electronic, mechanical, photocopying, recording, scanning, or otherwise without written permission from the publisher. It is illegal to copy this book, post it to a website, or distribute it by any other means without permission.

Karema McGhee asserts the moral right to be identified as the author of this work.

Designations used by companies to distinguish their products are often claimed as trademarks. All brand names and product names used in this book and on its cover are trade names, service marks, trademarks and registered trademarks of their respective owners. The publishers and the book are not associated with any product or vendor mentioned in this book. None of the companies referenced within the book have endorsed the book.

Second edition

Book 2

Table of Contents

ASANA ENERGY & ME 1

WHAT IS ASANA ENERGY? 3

THE SEDUCER OF MEN 7

THE BEGGAR 19

WOMEN WHO RULED THE MEN 27

SELF INVENTORY 37

EMOTIONAL FEARLESSNESS 39

HOW TO DEVELOP FEMININE CHARM 51

THE FEMININE MIND 59

THE QUEENDOM 71

RAGE 91

DELAYED GRATIFICATION 95

MOVING IN UNISON 99

THE CONNECTION 107

ABOUT THE AUTHOR 109

Asana Energy & Me

To begin any undertaking, a person must first work it out in his or her mind the thought, what is it that I'm trying to accomplish here? This complete work is made up of 3 parts, mind, body & spirit with the purpose of creating a definitive guide to feminine power and seduction. Part 1 is the introduction of Asana energy and uncovering the deep parts of your own energetic being. Part 1 will not only introduce us to Asana energy, but it will also uncover just what energy we've been working with.

What Is Asana Energy?

To be a woman is to be a divine force in cooperation with divinity.

This co-creating with source energy gives us the right to call on our Godship / Goddess energy, femininity or otherwise our divine powers.

Our African ancestors didn't leave much to the imagination as they were very vocal in handing down oral traditions.

They've left behind many points of reference if ever we are to be confused about who we are and what we are to become.

The temple walls of ancient Egypt give us examples of feminine energy and sisterhood as it relates to femininity.

We can look to Het Heru for beauty tips, sensuality and femininity, we can observe the divine sistership of Ast/Isis and Nebt/Nebhet.

The beautiful Yoruba people of Nigeria have given us the beauty of Oshun. We have the traditions of Yemaya, they've left no stone unturned when it comes to the understanding of the divine feminine spirit.

The ancestors have left us so much that there was no need for another name for expressing feminine power. This is because the world over, every tradition speaks to the ultimate feminine spirit. The Greeks have Aphrodite. The Buddhists have Kuan Yin which is the Egyptian equivalent of Isis. The Irish have Eriu, and the list goes on.

So, let's assume that there are thousands of names throughout the history of life and living that speaks to the feminine power, and I decide to add the perfect one to the list. Talk about Leo-ship here. Here's why I decided to add Asana. Asana has one thing the ancient at some point in history decided to change. We'll discuss this in my next book, but to give you an idea, Asana energy is complete. She's the one

Goddess energy that does not need masculine energy to be complete. She was neither created from the masculine, nor for the masculine. She was not created to serve him, nor to be in debt to him. She owes him nothing as it relates to her existence. In fact, neither him.

The way I see it, both the masculine and the feminine are but representations of the Earthly laws in line with what the ancient Chinese called the Yin & Yang. Both opposites of the same energy, hence that of itself divinely reflected, equally co creators.

For what I've come to understand about men as I've helped support hundreds of women over my 20 years of Holistic Healing, men are constantly seeking refuge of the feminine. It's almost as if the energy is trying to return back to that into which it came. The urge to be near her, to breathe her, to smell her, to feel her, and for most all men, to travel within her heaven.

I liken the sexual act as a divine marriage agreement to reach heaven together. I liken the spiritual connection a man has with a woman as the road map they will both use to get there.

The fact that men will start wars for just a taste of heaven leads me to believe that it is Asana who truly has the power here in this Earthly realm. Contrary to religious dogma, Asana is what he's after. The masculine is on a quest to return to God - the woman. Asana energy is creation itself; the goal of the masculine is to reconnect with the energy of all creation.

Asana energy attracts the masculine energy simply just by being.

Asana energy creates the created. She does not need to beg, borrow, steal, fight or otherwise chase the masculine because as water reaches its own level so will a mate find his Asana.

The best part about this idea is - she decides what's next and she decides just how much of the next he'll get to enjoy. The rules are hers and once she understands this, she will activate her sacred divine powers and any man she wishes to have will be hers. These rules not only apply in love, romance and living but in business, trade and negotiations.

The Seducer Of Men

Authenticity is the groundwork and the Jena se qua for the seducer of men. Beauty is secondary. The body, its shape, the curves, the mounds and the lines are catching to the eye, but it's the Jena se qua, which captures the man's soul.

Let me tell you the story of a woman who went by the name of Asana. Asana was a dark-skin woman, long dark hair, pretty long and slender legs, full arms, soft hands and manicured nails. She stood 5 feet tall on a small framed body with a full bust and equally wide shoulders. Some say she possessed an accent foreign to her native land, one - uniquely her own. A mysterious woman from the island of Tortola. Legend has it that her beauty was not in her physical features at all. Those who have experienced her say she captured their souls with her effervescence. One now - lonely suitor suggests that something magical had come from her breath while he was asleep in her bosom. He says he felt cold air coming from the bow of her lips and that it traveled a short distance to the top of his skull. The cold air transmuted into some sort of halo around his head which penetrated a pleasure providing sensation that traveled down his spine and into his sacred body parts. He says, "It was electric, but cold, electric but soothing." He believes the energy she transmitted that night was the life force itself. He feels it now even still, 8 years later. He's been on a quest to experience the magic he had while in Asana's presence but says no other woman has been able to activate that part of his soul.

If we are to look at Asana and do so without all the facts, we assume she was just a lucky woman with some sort of magical power over men.

The story I share above is to challenge your own understanding of your own divine feminine power. If for one second you thought Asana to be a rare breed of women whose power was linked to something supernatural, then this chapter is for you. If for one moment you believed Asana existed and was a legend because she existed, the next 100 words or so is for you.

First, let's understand that every woman is Asana. Deep within her, she is Asana. Before and after the hurt, disappointments, betrayals and the many tragedies of life, she remains Asana. It's the switch that activates the frequency of her pitch.

Asana is a fictional character that I created to describe a woman in total control of her divine feminine power.

The name Asana means powerful and complete.

Nothing added, nothing needed, she's complete.

The name alone embodies the nature of a woman who has divinely mastered her own inner strength. She's in control of her power and not ruled by her emotions. Asana is the woman who is not afraid to lose, not afraid to be alone. In fact, just like the warrior women of yesteryear, she looks at fear straight in its face and challenges it with the "faith power" she carries within her womb. She's fully alive in her body and every inch of her body is fully occupied by her spirit. This is the beginning of her divine feminine power.

What makes Asana the seducer of men is quite simple. She's the definition of femininity. Men love and can hardly resist femininity. They are always seeking a higher vibration of femininity and always seeking to experience what I call Asana.

Their search is never failing and always in need of reconnecting with that God/Goddess energy, hence why it's extremely difficult for a man to ignore a beauty when she passes by, even if a slight glance would result in a slap. That chance he's willing to take. The risk of checking out a woman who has entered a party possessing femininity and sensuality is a risk worth taking. Even when the odds of being found out are high. A small watching, a quick study, a moment's observation, a gentle scan, erotic thoughts, or imagery is all that he needs because, for the masculine male, seduction doesn't start with sex. It's in the presentation of the woman. The fabrics, the color, her smell, It's in her, and if a quick look would satisfy his hunger then the seduction was complete. He's satisfied. Now many women get upset, feel disrespected, throw tantrums and even get into fights with their mates because they've caught them eyeballing, watching, or otherwise checking another woman out. Let me save you a lot of time. When Asana energy walks into a room, the Wife, the Mother of his children, the Pope, cannot and will never stop a male from wondering, looking, desiring, or attempting to take a look at least. Asana energy is commanding; nothing can stop that. It's mother nature at work and if you're fighting with your husbands & boyfriends, about the wandering eye, beloved, you'll be fighting for life, and the battle is as good as lost.

The wandering eye is not only natural to an extent, but for an unsettled heart, it's a tell-tale sign that he's seeking rescue from Asana energy. Some men suffer from sexual addiction, promiscuity, infidelities, and emotional cheating outside of their relationships. The urge needs and desires to connect with Asana is a lifelong quest for many men. I liken that to the need to connect with source/creator energy—the desire to experience God.

Now you can call Asana, the God/ Goddess energy, you can call it femininity, you can call it feminine power, you can call it any of these things, but never call it promiscuous, never confuse it with sexuality or sex, never reduce it to a sheer attraction. Those things vibrate at a lower frequency.

Asana energy is different. It's grown and sure of itself; it stands out from a crowd and never yells, but is always seductively loud. It's the energy that the masculine cannot resist. For some, the power is alluring, pulling, attractive and can be dangerous if not managed. It's a softer version of eroticism colliding with provocative, but it's neither of the two. It's the stardust energy oscillating from a woman's heart chakra. It's the cosmos tightly knitted in the depths of her womb. It's the wave patterns printed on the tip of her Tepithemet and the waters that flow divinely between her legs. The oscillation creates an energy wave that transmits electric current from her energetic field outward. This energy can be felt up to 20 - 30 feet outside of her physical body. If Asana is completely present during sexual exchange, this energy can be the giver of life. It's pure source energy, the same energy required to fully transform a penetrated egg into a child.

The energy starts to show up in us at about age 17; we develop it as we experience life. Some of us are more than others, but those of us in our Asana period of life have mastered the duality of power. Those of us on our journey to Asana-hood are battling hundreds of years of feminine oppression. We are at war with pushed political agenda and up against a larger machine that teaches the ideology of "the stronger woman," The idea that softer is weak, that seduction is wrong and immoral, and that femininity and sex are synonymous. Women are afraid to be themselves. They are afraid to be all that being a woman has created them to be. Although afraid, most of us are curious.

We're searching for the answers; we need the elders, we are seeking to meet the woman within our own soul. There's a divine urge for us to meet this energy within. The problem is. No one's sharing the ancient secrets. No one's sharing the stories of the huts, of the village, of the women. Not until today.

Let me introduce you to the elder created in the story of Asana. She's the elder responsible for providing Asana with the internal road map that unlocked her power. She's a quiet woman always sitting in the shadows of a crowded room unless the music is grounded in drumbeats and saxophone notes. She's a large hip-swinging woman using her rhythm to exaggerate her walk. She carries around the bottom that jiggles as if it's dancing on its own. Rhythmically, she's aware that her round bottom and large hips are attention-grabbing, so to delight her onlookers, she swings her hips to the sounds of Afrobeat playing in her head. She gets pleasure from people watching and dancing out of control with strangers. A fat Cuban cigar lays at the edge of her lips most times and her perfume muddles the atmosphere.

Elder Eden is from Cameroon; she's Cameroon Cameroon yet culturally conflicted. As her parents are from two different parts of the continent Africa, her father from Benin, and her mother from Cameroon, she's all spirit and all music, wise, and a legend in her own right. The villagers see her as a spinster, but never will they have the courage to call her that out loud. They say she'll rob a man blind of everything with no desire to bed him, only leaving him with the unfulfilled desire to be with her completely. Elder Eden teaches the young women of her village how to keep house, and she grooms them for marriage. The ironic thing is, she's never been married herself. She's been sort after since age 12, but a village elder advised her parents long ago not to interrupt her destiny. At 14 years old, Asana was traveling with her parents to Cameroon to do some mission work. A woman with a cigar walked up to her at the village's missions center and placed a strain of beads in her hands and told her to come back to the village the next day.

Two nights had passed, she had met with the woman and on night 3, Asana found it hard to sleep; something in her was keeping her awake. She tossed and turned, felt her legs go numb and allowed what felt like pain travel down her spine into her belly. A loud outburst of a cry that startled the entire village was just the beginning. She sat up, rocking back and forth, moaning in agony, begging for her mother to enter, asking for help, and pleading to the sympathy of those watching to remove the pain. A young boy was instructed to run down the road and get auntie. He pushed the onlookers out of the way on a mission to get the medicine woman of the village. His shoes flipped through the dirt as if a hundred soles had been dancing. His shirtless self-appeared at the door of elder Eden, and within a moment's notice she had calmed the pain Asana was feeling.

Young child arrived is your sacred monocycle. You are well on your way to experiencing this power I've known forever. Finish the rest of this emetica tea, and as you rest, I'll pour the ancient secrets into your soul.

Long ago was the first encounter of elder Eden, as Asana was now the age elder Eden was when she first met her, which felt like many moons ago. She untied a red string from around the unbound book given to her by elder Eden and opened it. The first words that appeared was the first part of her teaching.

First, chose if you are the hunted or the hunter. Second, based on that decision, chose if you care at all either way and lastly, focus all of your energy over the next seven years on developing your charisma.

Asana recalls her 21st birthday, and Elder Eden extended another lesson. It is better to know yourself than it is to want to control others. Take seven years beloved, to work on your self-control, and I can guarantee you a life of loving lovers who consistently seek you out.

The pages of the book were falling apart, but the lessons of how she had become the great Asana, was very much intact. The tears of remembering the mentor who developed her were happy expressions of life and living. To reflect on her 28th birthday, she recalls the laughter of elder Eden. The laugh contiguous enough to erupt a full stadium of people. Asana had told elder Eden of the story of a young prince from an Arab land who caught wind of Asana in Nigeria. For six years, he had fought for her only to be left to marry a much less confident and less alluring woman. Asana, though compassionate in nature, laughed with elder Eden about never have to let the young prince enter her heavenly gates.

Nigeria is now the place Asana calls home; as life in the village is far behind her, she rests happily as a content woman at 40. The final lesson that elder Eden had given her was the driving force of her life. To seduce men, you must believe yourself—no convincing anyone. You must know who you are and believe the words you feed yourself daily.

The outro of chapter 1 will sum up what for sure is the title of the book manifested in word form but let's simplify this chapter for you. Know that Asana energy is within you. This book is elder Eden. Tortola, Cameroon, Nigeria and the village is all who take from this wisdom. Asana energy is necessary for women looking to be more than just a wife to a man. Asana energy is necessary to keep the masculine energy engaged. It's the Asana energy that allows a woman's voice to be the loudest voice in her own head. It's Asana energy that keeps a woman confident, feminine and easy-going.

As a God energy, or Goddess energy, a source energy, express it however you like. When we enter our Asana period of life, we realize that we are complete. The natural desire for the masculine is to want to connect with God/woman again. It's at this point in our adult life, that we no longer fight for love and adoration. We know how to create it.

This mystery is what they are after. Intuitively they can feel something different about a woman who is in her Asana period of life. To be a seducer of men, one must be in her Asana period of life. Until then she's the beggar.

The Beggar

To gain pity from your lover instead of adoration is the worst place to find refuge.

In her words;

Twenty-one years of marriage and just like that, he threw it all away with an 8-month affair. Each night, he lies in bed next to me dreaming of this woman, kissing my lips after kissing hers, having sex with me with no emotion, no passion, no love, all while after making love to her. My only question to him after finding out was - please give us another chance. Twenty-one years is on the line; I'll forgive you if you would just give us another chance. He simply said, he loves her, and I haven't heard from him since.

This story is so unkind, but if we are honest with ourselves, we have all been in this position in some way or another. Your heart has beenbroken; you've been betrayed, your trust has been taken for granted and most importantly, the one you love, loves another.

By some strange reason or a set of unfortunate events or by what feels like default, you've moved from the wife position to the beggar positions. At one point, you were the love interest he pursued and courted, but just like that - you've become the beggar.

The beggar energy is the physical manifestation of a woman totally trying to control the outcome of a decision made by an unwilling partner.

The beggar energy wants to convince. It needs to dictate; its motivation is the idea that a victory is possible even if the circumstances are not plausible. To talk her lover into making a decision otherwise is the beggar. Even in victory, the beggar will rarely be content with the victory, because deep within her intuition tells the truth about the circumstances. So even if she fools other people, she can never really fool herself. This makes for a terribly insecure person, most often plagued by self-esteem and trust issues. The beggar who wins knows that the victory is but short-lived, but the fear of losing is far too great to face, so she pretends the victory was worth it.

The beggar who struggles with a victory, will scream pick me, pick me with her actions. Not knowing that the beggar energy is repelling, so attraction from the masculine is a futile feat. Screaming pick, me, pick me, will never work to change the mind of a man. That energy will never activate his greater self. The beggar energy will never result in divine connection, and so just as we've learned in chapter one, he'll remain seeking Asana energy.

Calling repeatedly, sending angry text messages with no reply, sending emails and pictures of a much better time, following him on social media, sending gifts only to be ignored, and still, the rejection remains; this is the beggar in action. To be ignored is internalized as being rejected and the feeling of being unwanted feels insurmountable. Perhaps denial keeps a heart open to begging, but one cannot deny the pain one receives by unrequited love. Rejection is a terrible feeling, I know. To feel unwanted by someone you've invested time, energy and love into feels terrible. Part of you has so many unanswered questions; perhaps you feel closure would help. One part of you feels lost, disappointed, angry, sad even. Maybe you're even questioning revenge in some manner, but most of what you feel if we are to keep it simple and in line with understanding where you are, most of what you are feeling is fear. You are feeling the physical manifestation of fear. The heart palpitations, the tears of rage, sadness and pain are by-products of Fear. Fear teaches us the most important lesson about ourselves. It exposes the areas we are most unhinged. This exposing of things as they are is a process of uncovering, and this process is at times a heart-breaking experience. In some cases, before we've identified the cause of the pain, we spend many moments grieving what we feared to begin with. The fear of losing all that we've worked so hard for, the fear of losing it to someone else, the fear of being rejected, of being alone, of considering what's next, the realization that these are actual things we'll face as a result of the set of circumstances in front of us is one scary place to be in. Although scary, these are actually very valid questions that reach levels of anxiety when paired with dealing with an unwilling lover.

If you've ever been in the position of the beggar, it's important to understand that both the Beggar and Asana energy cannot occupy the same space. You're either Asana or the Beggar. You're either attracting or repelling. If you're the beggar right now, all is not lost. You must get honest with yourself if you want to heal. I bet far before the betrayal, far before the disappointment, long before the affair happened, your Asana energy had left and at some point, you've been on autopilot, perhaps only operating out of fear.

Most often in relationships, we get so busy pleasing we forget what it feels like to be pleased. We forget how it feels to be served because we are so busy serving and if we are not careful we even forget ourselves.

Let me share a quick story with you about pleasure and how Asana approached being pleased.

Asana invited a hopeful lover to her home; she ushered him to her altar. There the music was in line with moods coming from a Zen like Yoga retreat. The smell of Jasmine and ylang-ylang was in the air, and the red, pink and white candles flickered ten separate flames. Asana began chanting; she took a deep breath in, placed her hands on her belly and leaned forward in a trance-like state. Her hopeful lover enjoyed watching her; curious and entangled in her mystery, he closed his eyes to give thanks. A sweet and gentle kiss from Asana widened his eyes as she used her tongue to delicately place a saffron strand in his mouth. She later placed her left hand softly on his chin to close his mouth, grabbed his right earlobe in between her right thumb and pointer finger, gave it a firm tug, and whispered into his eardrum -serve me.

One hour had passed and her body had been covered in sweet almond oil. Her lover had covered her body with the pressure of his hands, the kneading of his elbows and a massage for her tired muscles with his fingers.

Asana had completely surrendered to her own feminine power, and thereby activated his masculine energy. To thank him for sharing his energy, she rewarded him with a note of a possible next encounter in his left hand. Satisfied and content both Asana and her hopeful lover had both exchanged a level of intimacy only witnessed by a woman owning her true femininity and in true masculine form, her hopeful lover was happy to oblige.

This story of Asana and her ability to allow the masculine to serve her speaks more to her ability to ask for what she wanted and less about her sensual allure. She invited her lover to taste pleasure; he was pleased and so the natural thing for his exchange to be equal was to give her pleasure.

To wrap up this chapter, evaluate your feminine charm, your allure and your overall energy and ask yourself an honest question. Ask yourself: Have I been all that I can femininely be? Proceed to the next question. Am I the beggar? This answer will empower you more than you know. If your answer is yes, do not be heartbroken. Understand that this is your healing moment, take all the time you need, but remember both Asana energy and the beggar cannot operate out of the same space. You are either Asana energy or the Beggar energy. You are either attracting or repelling either way; life will make you face the truth.

Women Who Ruled The Men

I'll take you on a trip back in time. Imagine it's the late 1800s and we're in Victorian London. Some of the great aristocrats, politicians and intellectuals of those times looked cross-eyed in a mystified way at a young woman by the name of Catherine Walters otherwise known as skittles.

Catherine Walters was born in 1839 in Liverpool and is remembered as one of the great courtesans of her time. In today's world view, she would be reduced to such names as a prostitute, escort or sex worker. However, this would be a wrong assessment of who she was as a businesswoman, a skilled horseman, a fashion trendsetter and a well sort after woman. It is said that she was paid handsomely for her encounters. There are stories documenting her love affairs, her lovers and how she amassed her fortune, but she has never publicly confirmed her lovers. She kept her lovers private. Legend has it that this was part of her allure. One such lover was King Edward VII who was King of the United Kingdom of Great Britain and Ireland and Emperor of India from 1901 until his death in 1910. Another was a writer and poet Wilford Blunt who obsessed tirelessly after her until his death.

As you can see, she attracted some of the most prestigious men of her time. They would not only buy her whatever her heart desired, including property and such, but they would fall madly in love with her. In a biography of her, author Henry Blyth wrote that she possessed the quality of being loved.

Catherine was not only a beautiful, well-dressed woman whose clothes were perfectly tailored to her body, but she was more than just a pretty face. You see, Catherine was also a legendary horseman. It is said that even women would stare for hours as she rode. Her skills were exceptional, and her sense of passion for riding opened many doors for her and garnered her respect for her sense of style and skill as a horseman. There is much to be said of Catherine, but this is where I end the story. You'll learn why shortly.

Catherine Walters

Next, we'll travel to 16th century India. I'm sure you're aware of the famous Taj Mahal. However, I would like to give you a few fascinating facts about its construction and shed some light on the feminine energy that sparked the inspiration for why it was created.

Commissioned in 1632 by Emperor Shah Jahan as an eternal resting place for his beloved wife Mumtaz Mahal, It has been seen as the ultimate romantic gesture.

I believe it's important to note that the name Mumtaz Mahal was not the birth name of Arjumand Banu Begum, which is Mumtaz's maiden name. The name Mumtaz came from the title Mumtaz Mahal Begum. This title was given to Mumtaz from Shah Jahan who married her at age 19. The very title was inspired by the said striking beauty Jahan saw in her. He was so enamored with her beauty that he gave her the title Mumtaz Mahal Begun which means, The Chosen One of the palaces. Seeing as though multiple wives were culturally appropriate in those times, being given the title Mumtaz Mahal Begun could have been seen as a victory over all the others.

Mumtaz had a 19-year marriage with the emperor and had given him 14 children. More than a few died at birth, and a few in early childhood, into which the 14th child resulted in her own death ironically. Although the Taj Mahal wasn't built until one year after her death, that was not the beginning nor the ending of their love story.

During their 19-year marriage the emperor was sure to cover her stately room in gold, award her the highest allowance of the other wives and trusted her with his affairs before anyone else. It is said that she was not only his confidant, but she also acted as his military advisor.

She accompanied him on missions and even travelled with him during some of the most difficult times. One being her last pregnancy. The one that lead to her death. Legend has it that her last words to the emperor as she was taking her last breath was for the emperor to make a promise. That promise was for him to build a place most beautiful for all the world to see. As she took her last breath, the emperor cried, broken-hearted with yes as his response.

The emperor held steadfast to his promise as he had lost the one woman he could trust with his life, his people and his kingdom. He was sure to make good on it. He mourned her death for two years in despair. The mausoleum where she would rest is one of the 7th wonders of the world; it's safe to say he kept his word. Some say the majestic, ethereal mausoleum was built not of love but from grief. I would like to believe it was from both.

There are a few character traits of Mumtaz not often discussed as she was bilingual and spoke multiple languages. She was a skilled diplomat with a sincere and deep concern for the poor and under privilege. She possessed a fierce fire that the emperor found just lovely, so much so that he gave her the seal of the land which is the highest honor anyone could get. The Mehr Uzaz was the Royal seal and solidified her as the Mumtaz Mahal. The great love for all the ages.

Mumtaz Mahal

Our final journey leads us to ancient Egypt. We're heading straight to the hem of one of history's most seductively powerful, alluring, cunning and almost mythical in nature - women of all time, Queen Cleopatra.

One of the world's most famous queens known the world over, Queen Cleopatra was able to conquer her lovers as a means of domination, political security, power, strength and femininity. She singlehandedly captured her lovers with her wit, charm and her fearlessness.

With men like Mark Anthony & Caesar, one would never debate her ability to make her lovers fall to her feet. Her scandalous affair with Anthony would bring much trouble to the Roman Empire and stirred war, but in the end, she controlled not just her lovers but also her choice in how her life ended, I would like to think.

The woman behind the myth is much more interesting. It is said that she spoke over a dozen languages, was highly educated and enjoyed mathematics and astronomy. It is no wonder she would be the kind of woman Caesar himself would risk it all for. He even went as far as having erected a statue of her in the temple of Venus Genetrix.

After the death of Caesar, she left Alexandria and later married Mark Anthony. The two lovers died a death people debate being either a planned tragedy in great solidarity or the tragedy of the fall of the Roman empire. Either way, Mark Anthony's thoughts of Cleopatra dying without him lead to his suicide and Cleopatra's death was as a result of the same thing. It appears the two lovers couldn't stand the idea of not knowing if the other had died without the other. Cleopatra, the woman, was loved greatly by the men she went for; never could they deny her wishes, not simply because she was the last pharaoh of Egypt, but because she used her feminine powers over even great men.

Now that we've discussed just a few women who've ruled the men by simply being the best version of themselves, I'm hoping that you, the reader can see a common thread through the women discussed. Each woman had a sense of personal style, but most importantly, they had a learned spirit. They've each had a skill they mastered. Each had something to offer besides beauty. Each woman listed was famous for something other than their beauty. To master the masculine, you must first master something other than the masculine. Your desire for self-mastery is femininity expressed. Women who skill themselves become interesting, women who master the art of developing feminine charm will activate within them their Asana energy.

To learn a skill, to master a skill, to develop it, refine yourself, define yourself is to be unlike the ordinary. Men will cause wars for extraordinary women.

Are you extraordinary or ordinary? The ordinary becomes boring really quick, and just as the blade of grass that will break through the concrete, the man will seek out true Asana energy regardless of the circumstances.

Today is the perfect time and space to understand that for each lover you attract or repel, each one is a divine reflection of where you are in your feminine development, your true personal power or lack thereof. You have the power to have men at your feet, but you must learn first how to be great at being you. The real secret is understanding that the goal is always enhancing you; men falling at your feet is natural and for sure just secondary.

Self Inventory

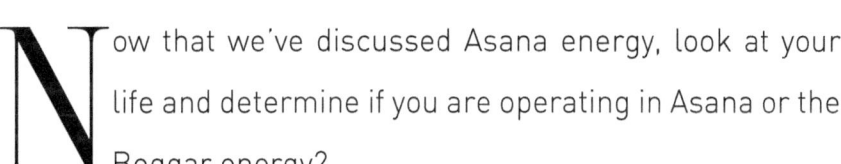

Now that we've discussed Asana energy, look at your life and determine if you are operating in Asana or the Beggar energy?

Here are some self-inventory questions to help you identify where you are. Please keep in mind that this is your work. Do not be afraid of the answers and be open to facing some hard truths about how you choose to love. The reason I say choose is that here, we believe in a fair, loving exchange between two consenting adults. The keyword here is fair. Asana energy is not evolved enough to love unconditionally here in this realm. Herself love doesn't tolerate disrespectful behavior, nor can she accept below-average treatment in exchange for simply loving someone. Asana has boundaries and her affection and her choice to exchange with another human simply rides on his ability to prove that he honors each encounter. The reason that is, is to protect her sanity, her femininity and herself. Take a deep look at the questions below. Write out your answers and reflect.

1. Have I been successful at love and romance?
2. Does love seek me out no matter where I go?
3. Have I had to end some pretty good relationships to focus on my journey?
4. Have I no trouble setting standards and boundaries in dating and always stick to my guns?
5. Am I good at letting things go when things are over?
6. Am I always being dumped by my lovers?
7. Have I never really been loved before?
8. Am I yet to experience a true courtship?
9. Have I never been proposed to before?
10. Am I sure that love is not meant for me?
11. Am I not a lovable person?
12. Can't I ever depend on anyone?
13. Do I often times find myself needing closure?
14. Do find rejection hard to accept?
15. Do I often make excuses for my lovers' bad behaviors?
16. Am I a very forgiving lover?
17. Have I experienced childhood trauma, some which are unresolved?

Emotional Fearlessness

To ask someone to be everything you need is asking far too much. It's a dangerous game that can lead to an unfulfilled life. In this chapter, we'll challenge your understanding of self-esteem, self-worth, resilience and your level of emotional fearlessness by way of discovering and uncovering just how emotionally stable you are.

As we develop into our very own level of emotional fearlessness, we not only encourage others to do the same, but we create healthy relationships with boundaries, standards, a sense of calm and overall wellbeing. We begin to learn how to create the love we seek from within and the anxiety, depression and heartbreak that comes from trying to control others naturally falls away. We become less codependent and much easier to love, and most importantly, our chosen lovers no longer must carry the burden of having to be everything we need.

You see, self-esteem, self-worth and resilience are all examples of inner healing and growth. They become personality characteristics used to describe just how emotionally evolved a person we've become.

I used the word become because to become resilient is a process of learning and unlearning. It's a process of falling and getting back up. To become self-esteem proficient is also a learning and unlearning process, drowning out the outer noise learning how to trust your inner voice. The process of becoming is a slow and steady process of refinement and self-discovery.

We've been living our lives asking people to be more for us than we are for ourselves; expecting people to love all the broken pieces and backfill all the empty spaces. In fact, not only have we done this repeatedly, but we live in a culture that helps to foster such madness. In Western culture, here in America's movies, TV, magazines and social media are the person's developmental environment. It's the incubator program for today's people. The media is now developing people - shaping how they think, behave and engage with one another, long ago that was the job of University's, travel nature & reading.

Today, it's mass media that creates the façade and expectations of perfection. This process leads people to crave status and acceptance. The tool of mass media programming has been a horrible example of developing an entire nation of entitled, yet afraid people. If we are honest, it can feel like a huge failed social experiment. The outcome being a nation of people seeking validation, likes, attention and confirmation of who they are. Scared of rejection and failure, unsure, doubtful and dependent on others, stressed anxiety-filled and looking for a lover to fill in all the gaps that life, living and the media has created.

This wheel of dysfunction creates a world of emotionally immature people. A nation of people who've learned how and whom to love by way of manipulation & control and not by cooperation and respect. It's adulting in the most dangerous of ways. It's a road map that ends in the depths of a cul-desac. One that disables a person's willpower, free-thinking and emotional fearlessness.

Let's chat a second about emotional immaturity and what it is. Emotional immaturity is often the thoughts, ideas, and state of being/feeling emotionally fragile. On the surface level being emotionally fragile can be a learned behavior, a lack of developmental support, or untrained conflict and resolution faculties. To be emotionally fragile is best describe as being emotionally unstable at times. To be easily disrupted emotionally by one or more circumstances without considering all the facts, Random mood swings relating to unrealistic expectations of others. Uncertain behavioral changes as a result of what is internalize as rejection, becoming angry at someone but refusing to express or communicate what angered you, and becoming upset and angry at someone because they failed to do what you expected them to do even though you never communicated your expectations. Moving into a dark space because of any of the above aforementioned reasons could be a sign of emotional immaturity.

However disruptive, being emotionally fragile at one or more times in one's life is completely natural. However, deep within the psych of a person who oftentimes exhibits emotional instability, for longer periods or as a part of his or her personality, this could be a sign of a much more serious mental health issue or perhaps a sign of past trauma, and this is how they manage.

Here we'll suppose it's surface-level only, giving us access to regaining power over our emotional well-being in an easier way. The later requires professional help which I encourage even those not needing help to consider.

Let's dive deep. Have you ever felt emotionally fragile? Be honest with yourself. Where were you mentally, physically? Do you remember if there were circumstances surrounding how you felt and why? Can you recall that feeling?

If I was a betting woman, I would dare to say, it was the most vulnerable you've felt. To take it a step further, I would dare say, you've felt at your lowest, maybe uncertain, doubtful or fearful about the future. You see, these feelings are coming from the same space. The same place in your mind, in your body and almost undoubtably from some scared moment in time. The reason I said from the same moment in time is because I believe the body keeps score.

The body keeps score ideology is dear to me. I've been practicing holistic health for over 20 years, and this quote is from a book by Dr. Bessel van der Kolk. In his book, the body keeps score Dr. Vessel Van der Kolk focuses on the impact childhood trauma has on the growing mind and how well we manage our emotions after the trauma. He shares his theory that we can be hurt, but we can heal. I've shared this sentiment for my entire 20 years of helping people navigate through health and wellness. I know that trauma is a fact in life. Each one of us has experienced some sort of trauma at some point in our lives, but what separates those emotionally fit or emotionally fearless from the emotionally immature is how and if we move forward inspite of the trauma. The troubling thing about trauma is if we are not careful, we can become imprisoned by the trauma and never fully evolve past it. We will be enslaved by it. Tied to it, and over the years unhealed - we become it.

In his book "The Body Keeps Score," Dr. Bessel van der Kolk says that severe trauma is 'encoded in the viscera' and demands tailored approaches that enable people to experience deep relief from rage and helplessness."

The viscera is the main cavity of the body, mainly comprising of the heart, lungs, intestines, digestive area and stomach. In agreement with Dr. Kolk, the trauma we felt gets stored in this part of the body and is repeated in what is known as the viscera feelings, known the world over as "gut feeling,"

If we are to assume that Dr. Kolk is correct in his theory and also consider that most people are taught to trust their gut feeling and act on them, it could be a scary thought to think of the impact this could have on a person's relationships or on their lives.

If Dr. Kolk's information is correct, then most of the information stored in the gut is past hurt or trauma, and people are using feelings to make important decisions. This sounds like a flawed way of living if we are to consider that what we are indeed responding to is a repeat of the past and not necessarily a true representation of what might be the reality.

I suggest we teach people how to use reasoning skills, using emotional intelligence and help people uncover the self mastery skills required to use logical thinking. Especially considering that most of us are using a flawed gut-feeling approach to life and living, we might also want to reconsider the whole idea of trusting your gut completely when unhealed trauma exists. In fact, most of what emotionally immature people feel as gut instincts or an inner knowing is actually a projection of their own inner fears and or trauma.

When you deal with your hurt, your trauma and your past, you can begin to learn to trust your ability to think things through. To really be able to think things through is a sign of emotional intelligence. This can transform into emotional fearlessness, but only after we learn to trust that emotions are but messengers only. We must learn that we can indeed control what and how we feel in response to an evoked emotion. We can decide if we are to react or respond upon feeling any kind of emotional disturbance.

To become emotionally mature requires work. To become emotionally fearless means that numbing the pain becomes less and less necessary. We learn how to navigate difficult times, and we face our emotions with intelligence and act accordingly. Not react, but act.

In today's world, more prescription medications are being written now more than any other time in history. This is all to help the masses deal with some form of anxiety or depression, trauma and heartbreak. We spend more time researching and developing medicine to help numb the realities of life than we do creating classes to teach people how to use their mind power to overcome, how to use their intellect and emotional fearlessness to navigate through it. In today's times, we've made more advances in technology than we've had in human behavioral sciences.

As you learn to deal with the fact that life will have some horrible endings, some sweet beginnings and some doubtful in betweens, you'll learn that navigating through trauma is a natural part of living and co-existing with humans. Now the question becomes, but how?

The next level

I've learned that over the years the world's most sought-after women were women who lived on their own terms, made their own rules and designed a life for themselves others wanted in on. These women truly had no desire to live for others, nor did they seek others for validation. These women enjoyed more than anything the natural allure of being themselves completely and unapologetically. It's as if they were all in on a big secret, that secret being - focus on becoming you, and all the world would like to join in. That's the message as we wrap up this chapter.

To ease you into the most healing part of this book, we want to tap into what I call triggers. Triggers words or phrases are those things that either pull out the best in you or the worst in you. My mother would say, no one can bring out in you what wasn't in there to begin with. She would also say, never let a person make you feel different about who you are. It's these two things that bring about the next steps here in this book. It's important to note that everything ends and begins with you as it relates to your life. If the outside noise is louder than your own inner voice, then forever will you be a slave to your emotions.

A few discovery words or phrases below will get you thinking and also start you on your journey to emotional fearlessness, self-esteem and inner power. As you read the words below, take a moment to review the word or phrase and write the first thought that comes to mind. Don't think, just allow. After discovering the outcome of your writings, be sure to explore any deep meanings and check for patterns. As you uncover your writings, you'll discover that certain words either pull information forward or they can make us retract. It can be a beautiful thing to uncover unconscious thought patterns. The exercise below is using trigger words to uncover your innermost fears. Trigger words or phrases is a process used in marketing as a psychological process to get someone to act or react. It's also a process used in past regression therapy to uncover deep unconscious thoughts about a thing or circumstance. The most important part of this exercise is to allow your mind to be free.

Triggered words

Fat: _____

Yes: _____

Goals: _____

Dark: _____

Puppy: _____

No: _____

I love you: _____

You're crazy: _____

I can't: _____

Not now: _____

I don't trust you: _____

How To Develop Feminine Charm

At some point in your adulthood, you'll realize that what you required at age 19 is completely different at age 30. At least it should be a consideration. If by chance your needs haven't changed much over the years this is the perfect moment to consider - why not?

As we are growing into ourselves, it's important to remember refinement, development and change. If we do not allow experience, wisdom and knowledge to shape us, then it is plausible that we have denied our own growth. Perhaps it's fear, the fear of change could be stopping our growth, but with that it also impedes our experiences, and the levelling up of those experiences. If it's anything stopping our growth, it's also factual that we're going about and doing things the way we've always done it. With this understanding, it's a matter of nonfiction that our results have not changed over the years as well.

A woman looking to experience better from life, better from her mate, from the men she will encounter, will need to learn quickly that it's not about who she is that is energetically appealing. It is more about who she is becoming. A woman who embraces self-development, refinement and change is a woman in charge of her life regardless of the circumst-ances. A woman who can challenge her own thought process is on the road to mastering Asana energy.

Seduction, allure and to get the curiosity of a true masculine male is what you have, how much you have and all that you've accomplished, but it's more in the mystery in who you are to become.

The mystery for women is her true superpower. The unknown, the intangible, the spontaneity of what she'll do next.

To learn a new sport, learn how to bowl, play golf, race cars, paint, play an instrument, write a screenplay, dance, sing, sew, decorate, make jewelry, or simply do something, anything, but just be pretty, learn how to do something, become great at it, hold it close and allow the passion for that thing to energize you, but keep it to yourself. That will take your feminine charm to the next level.

You see, women who do extraordinary things are revered, women who have developed some sort of discipline are admired and those who have a fulfilled life without a partner are sort after. If you are looking to change the landscape of what your life has been and what it is to become you must learn something.

You must do something different. For those of us constantly allowing ourselves to evolve, the unspoken message to the world is, we are expecting greater. The world naturally responds as you wish.

Expecting greater is where you will first learn how to develop your own feminine charm. As a warning, if you've done things a certain way your entire life, this new way of thinking might challenge all that you know and may require a bit of courage on your part. You see, wanting more for your life requires self-reflection, realization and honesty. You have to have the courage to say to yourself that the way I love is not serving me, those whom I loved were not serving of my personal growth. I've allowed my old ways of doing things to stop my evolution as a woman.

Or if your story has been successful, then lead with that. However, moving forward will require you to do some things out of your wheelhouse. The first step is to challenge yourself by expecting greater from the lovers you allow in your life. But if you are expecting this, understand that this is an unspoken language you have by developing yourself into someone new. Someone new to you. Evolve, dear heart; this will send a message to the universe that you are indeed ready. Evolve, refine, and make new - the old you.

It's time to try something new. Have you ever thought about learning a new language? Bilingual women are intriguing. Multiple languages not only show just how evolved you are, how different from the rest you are, but the masculine will feel the discipline required to learn multiple languages and thus lead with showing you just how to discipline in his actions. He can be with you. It's an unspoken language. Have you ever considered learning how to play an instrument? Here's why I asked that to learn how to play an instrument, is to learn the art of seduction & feminine charm at the same time. The beauty of learning how to play piano, the manipulation of the keys, the suggestion of the cords, the delicate movement of the fingers, the effortless softness used to create a song that vibrates an entire room is sheer femininity without force. If you can learn to play just one song on the piano, you would have leaped years of etiquette classes; you would have made genetic changes within each cell of your body, allowing you to lean into the feminine charm. A few lessons will teach you to pose, placement, and how to energetically move into song. Feminine charm is simply a woman who's learned how to move in song with everyone she encounters.

To be charming is an art you can develop. Some people are naturally charming because of their personality and charisma. Others have never developed it over the years. The reason you'll find an entire chapter on how to develop feminine charm is that I understand the mystical powers of a charming woman and I want every last one of you to master and develop this side of you. I want you to understand that feminine charm equals attraction, it's the influence that can lead you to affluence. You must develop it now if you are looking to improve your life. Everyone loves a charming person, including the masculine.

Most charming people are enjoyable to be around, they are positive, upbeat, caring, loving and many of them are great listeners.

To develop your feminine charm, you must learn to become a very good listener. You must learn how to be most interested in other people and their stories. Allow them to feel your genuine care and interest, invite them to share, truly listen, be quiet, look them in the eyes, listen with your whole body as they share, pay attention and respond in sincerity. Many people want their stories heard, but Asana energy captures the heart by not needing that moment. For Asana, it is much more important to learn about others.

You must remember, everyone loves the sun, this will remind you just how energetic you should be. The positive vibes people feel in your presence will make them want to experience more of your upbeat attitude. This will get you more invites than you could ever imagine, because the truth is, no one wants to be around a grim person, the sun is always much more fun. Remember to be light and easy, not too harsh, loud, rude or disrespectful. Remember to constantly be evolving and learning new things. These things will make you unforgettable, irreplaceable and much more valuable.

As you refine yourself as a sacred divine woman aware of her Asana energy, be mindful to always be learning but keep it to yourself. Let your next class be an etiquette course, a language course, a dress for success class. Allow yourself to be teachable and dive deep into learning how to become a new you. That's the feminine charm. It's becoming a better you while learning, listening and vibing with all you encounter.

The Feminine Mind

The feminine mind is a playground for creative genius works, and today, I plan to show you how to maximize the unique and divine feminine power, feminine mystique, and the power of thoughts by understanding and tapping into the power of how you're wired.

The Western world is seeking equality amongst men and women. Some even believe that the genderless argument is better off a safer option to approaching neurosexism as it relates to the mind of both men and women, but let me break this hard scientific truth to you. We are not the same. Let me repeat that, men and women are not the same. Regardless of our biological makeup, the mind of a woman is systematically and energetically different from that of her male counterpart. I'm sure without a doubt that Neuroscientist Gina Rippon, the author of The Gendered Brain; The new science that shatters the myth of the female brain," would greatly disagree with my thoughts as it relates to how both men and women differ. She's much more qualified to make such a theory not only plausible but make it so. Most of what I understand, comes from behavior implications, history and science. For me, we must not forget basic biology, evolution and the environmental impacts on human behavior and cognition. Let me dive deep.

I believe that the book, The Gendered Brain proves a few points as it relates to brain capacity, size, facilities, etc., but for me, I believe it completely missed the mark as I explained above. It supports a more feminist approach to proving that there is no difference in the design, function and size of the human brain to support the genderless ideology, but it fails to prove that we share the same thinking and cognitive reasoning, it also fails to consider the impact socialization, thoughts, behaviors & environment might have on neurotransmitters and how the brain performs. For, me it leaves out the idea that the brain is trainable, teachable and responsive at best. New technology such as MRI's, etc., have discovered that there is some evidence pointing to inherent differences of both men and women and how we're wired, and I applaud and celebrate the idea that science can embrace those differences. In "Sex differences in cognitive abilities," written by Diane Halphern former president of the American Psychological Association, Diane writes; "At the time, it seemed clear to me that any between-sex differences in thinking abilities were due to socialization practices, artifacts and mistakes in the research, and bias and prejudice after reviewing a pile of journal articles that stood several feet high and numerous books and book chapters that dwarfed the stack of journal articles ... I changed my mind."

A thinking person would wonder why such a brilliant mind would consider a different thought. Still if we were to ask Diane herself, she would admit to the amount of insurmountable data that proved none of what I proposed above could be discounted.

You see Diane is a fantastic researcher, hence why she held her position with the American Psychological Association; she is a -consider the facts kind of woman, never leaving out what I believe to be one of the most important pieces of neuroscience and that is to consider biology. In fact

Neurobiology must be considered when we are looking at cognitive differences of both men and women, regardless if we are to believe that there are sex differences in the brain. Fact or fiction, here in Asana world, we will always consider biology first; stuck in the paradox of equality, we must consider the psychological and reasoning skills of a mother. We start with the woman.

Women, What Is Critical Thinking?

As I've researched and explored Dr. Diane Halphern's writings, speeches and online video interviews I'm convinced if we were to ever chat about Asana energy, she would be on board. I say that cheeky, but with some sort of wonder and vision forecasting. As we review her thoughts on critical thinking in an interview with Pshycophedia.com published on Feb 6th, 2017, I would like you to get your note pads ready; here's some good stuff you can use. Before we dive in, let's consider this one fact - we can all improve our critical thinking capabilities. Especially women, we'll learn why later.

According to Diane in that same interview published in Feb, she says that when you are thinking critically, you are using some of the particular skills of critical thinking, and you are using them in a way that's going to make it more likely that you're going to get the good outcome that you are looking for. It is in this statement that I give you this entire chapter. The

Feminine Mind. According to Diane, critical thinking is essential, and we'll learn just how to do that here.

If you've been one to react or act in or out of emotion, perhaps developing your critical thinking skills will move you closer to Asana energy, improving not just your relationships with the masculine but also improving your overall life experiences.

For most of our lives, we've destroyed relationships because of our understanding of the circumstances, much to which is backed by emotionally charged outcomes resulting in no use of reasoning skills but grounded deeply in how we've felt about the thing. We've developed a friendship, partnerships and businesses the same way, but this way of living is a coasting approach which leaves one constantly in fear.

Our way of living is deeply connected to fear because most of us have yet to develop our critical thinking skills. If we can tap into our mind power, process a thing without bias, but to at least consider correlation, consider the facts and intelligently use that to come to a conclusion, we would hold the power to creating the life we want.

Now the question becomes, just how do we do that? According to Diane, we can develop our critical thinking skills, and as a personal development addict, I'll share a few tools you can use to further explore and develop.

Here are 5 steps you can use to strengthen your skills.

1. Before responding, consider all the facts.
2. Consider if your facts are biased or fair.
3. Evaluate the evidence
4. Allow time for reflection
5. Conclude only after you've done the above.

To test your ability to do the above, I'll give you a few scenarios, and I want you to consider these things happening to you, how would you react, what should your reaction be, and what would be your next plan of action.

Scenario #1

Wife enters the bedroom at 10:47pm, and hears that her husband is on the line; she assumes it's a female because he's whispering. She can't make out the words, so she stands outside the master bathroom door listening, but within minutes, the call is over.

What is your response?

Please remember your critical thinking skills above.

In the above scenario, if your response would have been to walk in as normal with no suspicion, would that have been a fair assessment?

Would it have been a better assessment than the one the wife made by assuming her husband was on the other line with a woman?

Would you have accused the husband of infidelity?

In the above scenario, the husband was making arrangements for a surprise birthday party for his wife, and without all the facts, we could have been reacting. Using emotional maturity, we no longer assume; we use our critical thinking skills to decide. Past hurt or beliefs would have been the motivating factor of such a reaction, but Asana energy is focused, not easily angered and calculated.

Scenario #2

Boyfriend is making dinner for his new girlfriend, it's 9:50pm, while standing at the stove stirring the pasta, a blue light from his cell phone indicates a new message. He walks over to the phone, reads the message, turns the phone over, and walks back over to attend to the food. The phone goes off an additional three times. He ignores it. The new girlfriend says nothing, grabs her coat and leaves.

What would have been your response?

Please remember your critical thinking skills above.

Leaving without communication is a sign of emotional immaturity. Unfortunately, if your decision was to leave as she had, you would have been operating out of fear and not intelligence. Now would you have been exercising your critical thinking skills to the fullest if you had done this? Was there enough evidence to determine the conclusion that warranted leaving? Would you have addressed the turning down of the phone?

Here are two facts to consider about this scenario that you may not have. 1. New girlfriend means the relationship is new, and 2, he was making dinner for her.

Here are two facts you didn't know. 1, the text messages were from a previous failed relationship where he communicated to the extent, he had moved on with a new woman, and 2, ignoring the phone was fear. He feared that even though he put in 100%, that this snag that he could not control would ruin it for him. In fact, it did.

Scenario #3

While surfing the internet one evening, James's girlfriend of 2 years realizes that a Facebook notification popped up on the screen, curious she clicks the notification only to be brought to James's Facebook page, he unknowingly forgot to sign out. Straight to the inbox, she goes only to find five messages from his ex. Upset, and angry she storms into the living room screaming, why is she messaging you? James confused and clueless, asks for clarification, only to be met with further accusations. James goes to the computer to check and sure enough, it was what he thought it was; James runs back to the living room to explain that he never responded to the messages, not one time had he responded, but already in rage, she packs her clothes leaves only to return 8 days later.

What would have been your response?

Please remember to use your critical thinking skills.

Did the girlfriend have enough information to be angry enough to pack and leave?

Was there enough evidence to prove that James was unfaithful, or planning to be?

Was the girlfriend's anger about infidelity or the sheer fact that the ex was sending messages?

In this final scenario, there's one fact that you might have missed and that is there was no evidence that James was unfaithful. However, what James was held guilty of, was not responding to the messages. The girlfriend later asked after she returned," why didn't you tell her about me?"

The girlfriend wanted James to have responded that he was in a relationship, but because he hadn't, it was just as bad as cheating.

On James's end, he thought that ignoring was a peaceful and less harmful let down to the ex. One he really didn't care too much about explaining. For him, he was happy in his relationship, so ignoring took extra pressure off him.

With the above scenarios, we must take a moment to realize that some things are better said. However, some things are better unfelt. If we would have allowed all three ladies in each scenario time to develop their critical thinking skills, each one would have ended up in less headache for all parties involved, but because emotions ruled the mind, none of the ladies got what they wanted.

To understand the feminine mind, we must explore skepticism. Women tend to be skeptical not because the proof is positive but because of past experiences. Not because they've thought it all the way.

The Queendom

"The character of a woman who owns her Queendom is expressed in how she treats others, how she expresses her disdain or contempt and what she does with the power within her realm." A refined and confident woman is not afraid to exercise her authority and does it in such a way that respect is not only garnered, but it spreads like a virus amongst the masses, urging, teaching, summonsing and setting the stage for what is. Her power precedes her, and all that is at stake falls behind her. This is the Queendom."

- The Beginning -

Enigmatic was Elder Eden's smile as she stunned a young Asana by simply stopping a man in his tracks. Her objective was to show Asana how it was to be done. "Don't be so mystified, never be so mystified by anything with your eyes especially with onlookers watching them. Your eyes will tell your secrets and people will use them against you; guard your thoughts, and don't let them seep through your brown eyes. Unless of course, you know what you're doing, and its intentional."

Elder Eden gave a belly laugh while using the back of her right hand to sooth the concerned look on the young Asana's face. She gave her two pats on her cheek as if she was petting her and motioned her forward. Asana, now deep in thought, kept her mouth closed and walked behind the great artistry known as Elder Eden's backside. The thunder of her walk, the jubilee clapping of her thighs all sent waves throughout the village. She kept one hand on the small of her waist while swinging the other arm wide and swift. It was apparent to anyone approaching, move aside, move aside. None of which was mentioned by her. It was simply an act that needed not to be explained. The crowd would part as if she had split the people like Moses had done at the Red Sea. Everyone would just move aside. Asana watched in admiration. All the while learning the art of commanding your space.

He was the son of Chief Kulu, the wise chief of a nearby village. Chief Kulu was highly prized for his wisdom and insight; some say it rivaled the intuition of a woman. He was strong in voice and stature, quick to temper, but secretly had the heart of a lover. Twenty years earlier, he experienced his first heartbreak by Elder Eden, she abandoned their love affair after he had come to her with a dream. The dream as he told it, exposed her intentions of never wanting to marry him but wanting nothing more than political protection. She did not lie to protect his feelings when he confronted her, nor did she lie to protect her interest. She was honest and vowed never to see him again. It was the abandonment for Chief Kulu that plagued him; it wasn't her intentions. In fact, he couldn't wrap his thoughts around the idea that she didn't fight to save their love. In fact, what was more perplexing for him was the question - had she ever loved him? Although Elder Eden and Chief Kulu's relationship had ended 20 years earlier, she was not aware of the many times he secretly saved her life and the many years he spent wishing he could be with her.

Chief Kulu sought a powerful yet sweet woman with feminine skill much like Elder Eden for his son Kulu Aliyu who was of age and seeking a wife. Chief Kulu was sure if he could find a woman like Elder Eden to marry his son, he could be sure that his son would calm his mischievous and womanizing ways, bed a wife and produce an heir.

And to whom do you belong? Chief Kulu said firmly addressing a young Asana with an inquisitive look in his eye. Asana, out of breath from following the lead and fast pace of Elder Eden throughout the village, replies. "I belong to no man. I am a sovereign being and cannot be owned."

"So, you've taught her well." Chief Kulu responded looking at Elder Eden with concern. Are you proud of yourself? Did you create a carbon copy of yourself? Is this the nonsense you're spreading?

Elder Eden relaxed her shoulders, pushed forward her bust and stepped forward with her leg the same side as her heart was on, and responded, "Why did you summon me and my student?"

Chief Kulu repeated his question in a much more relaxed manner, now looking away from Elder Eden but expecting an answer.

Elder Eden widened her step and replied, "I simply teach tradition."

Out of the confines' shadows appeared a tall, dark, handsome, self-assured warrior with a voice as deep as the ocean and shoulders as wide as the horizon. He stepped toe to toe to Asana, and pronounced, I am Kulu Aliyu. His breath was easily absorbed by the small nostrils centering her beautiful face. She slowly took two steps back leading with her leg to the same side her heart was on, lowered her eyes a bit, but not her head flexed her cheekbones with a slight tilt to the left and gave a deep penetratingly energizing bat of the eyes. The seduction took all but three seconds. He was hooked; he was in.

"What is your name?" Kulu Aliyu asked while stepping back to give her space.

"I'm sure you know who I am; we were summoned. Is it unfair for me to assume?" Asana quickly recalled Elder Eden's teachings from moments earlier. Do not be so mystified by anyone with your eyes. She was aware and made sure to conceal her thoughts. While awaiting his response by staring directly into his eyes with a look that could convince the strongest of warriors to bow. With a deep snarly look, he replied, "It is unfair; share your name."

Elder Eden, quickly snatched Asana by the arm, walked her up to Chief Kulu, and motioned for her to stand firm. With a fierce fire in her belly, she belted out - "Not this one. You will not. She cannot. I will not. Are you done with us? Can we leave?"

Chief Kulu pulled from the hurt buried deep within his fractured ego and slammed his staff across the trembling ground below Elder Eden's feet. "You waste a young fertile life, you miserable woman. What should I do? He has seen her already. He already wants her. It must happen. It is tradition."

" She will devour him, is that what you want? She is gifted beyond my teachings, and she carries a sweeter nectar between her gates. He appears to be stronger than you, but she is more powerful than I. It's not tradition to pair a male honeybee with a woman like her. You are asking for trouble within your village." Elder Eden, lowered her head in submission, kneeled before Chief Kulu and asked for a pardon.

- The Plot -

"Asana? Have you steamed potted today?" Elder Eden standing with herbs of Stinging Nettle, Red Raspberry Leaf and

Calendula Flowers, while awaiting Asana's response. "Yes, Elder,

I fetched the herbs myself while at the market this morning. Elder, I'm interested in humbling the Honeybee." "He's quite the troublemaker elder, but I find him harmless. I would like to exchange a few moments, a few laughs; I would like to know him more. I'm asking for permission Elder, not to bed him; I want to learn more about the Honeybee?"

"Beloved Asana, I've saved you from the hurt a Honeybee male can give. You are not yet ready to handle the hurt a honeybee can give. Do you want to feel the sting? Are you sure?" "Elder, but you told the chef, I would be more than fine. Why now do you say I am not ready, what lesson am I missing, what am I not ready for Elder? I am Asana; you said that. What am I missing?"

"Asana, the male honeybee wants nothing to do with its lovers after he's gotten what he wants. The greatest feminine energy can fall for the charisma of the honeybee, but none can withstand the sting he gives to be free after. It's his nature to be free. His makeup is to be free, even free from love. He cannot love completely; his nature is to mate only. Not love. Do you understand what that means?" Elder Eden's face was full of concern, and it was at that moment that she realized that Asana had also been seduced by the power of the Honeybee, the Prince.

"Elder, Asana stuttered, Am I the great Asana?" Elder Eden responded, "Yes my love, you are, but tradition says if Asana meets the honeybee too soon, her power and beauty would be stripped from her. All things in time, beloved."

Month's had passed since Elder Eden & Asana had first met the chief's son Kulu Aliyu. However, in Asana's mind, she was preparing to see him again. She had not made any plans but wanted to soak up all the training that Elder Eden was willing to give. She remained humbled and vowed never to mention his name again to Elder Eden; although the thoughts of her humbling what she now called the strongest honeybee she had ever met plagued her, she vowed to keep it to herself.

"I'm here at the market getting my sacred herbs as instructed by Elder Eden. Do I owe you any explanation?" Asana in a firm yet gentle voice, responded to a hurried prince.

"Call me Prince Aliyu. You will be one of many for me, and you will love it. I've been waiting for the moment to see you again, and as nature would have it, here you are. Give me your name," he said firmly. "You're aware of my name. I must go." Asana bent gently to grab the edge of her long white skirt to ensure it wouldn't drag behind her, and grabbed her basket full of sacred herbs and slowly walked away without looking back. The prince was in awe. How could someone so beautiful, so feminine, so soft, so intriguing, be so direct and matter of fact? This was a challenging encounter for Prince Kulu Aliyu. He wanted her more now than ever. The women he's encountered have never had the courage or guile to challenge him in such a way, let alone dismiss him, by walking away without apology. Although she wasn't disrespectful in the tune of voice, she most certainly was in words. The Prince had never witnessed that side of a woman before, most of his experiences had been met with passive or agreeable women. Asana seemed not too impressed by his power, nor his position as the Prince, nor was she concerned about the possible repercussions of her dismissal of him. This would make things much harder for Elder Eden as the Prince reported back to the village immediately to discuss his desires to his father, the Chief.

- *The Conditioning* -

" Slowly, Asana, bend forward, lower your backside. Just a bit lower now. Release the muscles in your abdomen; before you insert it, make sure the gemstone is facing your lover. Hold the slimmest part and take your time. As it is going in, you are taking a breath inward. Breathe in beloved, now insert it. Remember to breathe. Great job love, slowly, slowly, slowly. Great. It's in. How does that feel? How does that make you feel?" Elder Eden surprised at the ease into which Asana had performed the "Great Miracle Love Ritual," as she had, she was satisfied, smiled in what she now understood was beyond her?

"Elder, Am I ready?" Asana asked. "Beloved soon, just remember, your lover is only to get a peek of this beauty, to see it with his eyes and wonder what's beyond the veil. You must not allow anything else. This ritual is only for the hard to capture, only for the lover you adore. Do you understand? Let him see with his eyes the beauty he can have. The idea here is to show him your sparkling magic without releasing your magic to him. Do you understand? The way to his heart is through his eyes! The way to his body is through his senses. Men must feel you outside of sex. Anyone who believes sex will awaken a man's higher self is mistaken. This ritual will work on the hardest of lover's beloved, but you must follow tradition.

"Elder, much like the Honeybee?" "Asana, yes, much like the Honeybee, but I tell you, we must learn a couple more rituals to prepare you for him. Especially "The Scented Bloom" ritual. You have most of it already, but we must go over what scents work best on what personality traits; as the male is concerned, we'll go down to the open field tomorrow before sunrise to witness the blooms. You'll select your favorite and we'll blend a signature scent for you on the eve of the equinox. Does that calm your interest?" "Yes Elder, so what now?" "Go clean up, relax your spirit, we have much to do before sunrise Asana, and for sure, this Elder is in need of plenty of rest."

- The Production -

"The wind is cool Elder, and I believe I've encountered my spirit scent. I'm so in love with the scent of the Jasmine flower. I can literally feel the scent blowing in the cool air. Just look at it elder, isn't it just a fine flower?" Asana in the most adoring voice, was trying to get the attention of a busy medicine woman like Elder Eden, but the Elder was busy connecting with spirit. She could hear Asana off in the background, but she wasn't listening. Her attention was on the blooms. Asana, so full of enthusiasm, kept at it.

"Asana, beloved, the Jasmine is the flower used by commoners. It's a fine flower beloved, but any woman looking to capture the hearts of an entire Kingdom, she cannot be common. Are you a common woman dear? Is that who you are? Do you want to smell like every other woman in every village from here to Timbuktu? All around the world, Jasmine is the flower of choice for women. You dear are no ordinary woman. You dear are the great Asana. Keep looking; we have plenty of time before the sun rises. Sink your feet in the soil of the Earth beloved and ask spirit to guide you. If spirit guides you to many, so be it, but I trust that spirit had not led you to the Jasmine flower alone; that was your ignorance and haste. Never jump in haste beloved, always have something to compare what you think is great too."

"Yes Elder, I understand, but the coolness of the air made it difficult to escape the inviting smell. I thought it was for me." "Environments can be tricky, much like the Honeybee, be easy and take your time."

- The Storm Brewing -

The sun had lit the sky bright enough for day to call its name across the horizon, and the lessons of the day had already penetrated Asana's dark skin. Elder Eden decided to allow Asana's original encounter with the Jasmine flower. Still it was the power of a nightshade that could either be a medicine or poison that made the Elder agree. The blend would be perfect for Asana.

Months had gone by; the village was calm. No hustle and bustle, no huge events, no marriages and no trouble. Just as the Elder was blending the Elderberry for syrup, the sun went dark for moments on in. This was nature's way of alerting the elder that it was indeed time for the Oshun cleanse. The Oshun cleanse happened each year around this time; the elder would get the women of age ready for an internal detoxification process.

This detoxification process was much more of a beautification/fertility season used to prepare the women for marriage and fertility. The elder would use fasting of the women, light deprivation along with herbs to stop the mensuration of the women for 60 days. She was sure that removing the women from their homes allowed them to be less stressed and more in tune with themselves. The elder used this time to teach, nurture and care for the women, all while recalibrating their sacred menses to ensure a 28-day cycle. This process made it easier for fertility. It was said that the women enjoyed their time with the elder, and no one dared complain about the sometimes-horrible herbal blends. The schooling had not only connected the women in solidarity, but the mystery of the sacred feminine could be found in how hormonally their cycles began to link up. One by one, each cycle would flip to the others. By the time the Oshun cleanse was soon to be over, all the women would cycle the same. The Elder was heard explaining this phenomenon to a chief. As she explained it, She in fact had no control over this syncing of the sacred moon cycles and that no herb in her possession would do that. As she explains it, this happening is completely normal for all women, as she told the chef, this is nothing to be mystified by. The woman herself is the mystery.

After the season, many of the women would be sent back to their homes ready to wed, keep house, bare and care for children. Generally, during the last week of the Oshun cleanse, the women would be jumping in excitement because life would ultimately change for them. Most of the women looked forward to permanently being gone from their family's homes and starting lives all their own, especially since being groomed by the Elder gave them the power to choose their husbands. However, this week would prove to be different at the Elders. During the night fall, a cavalry of men barged the land and sacred center Elder Eden created for the training of the women. They ransacked the place, destroyed the huts, burned the Elders garden and removed two women unwillingly. The message was clear. Someone was unhappy with the work the Elder was doing and making it plain.

By morning news had spread like wildfires while the Elder sat quietly in contemplation while smoking her cigar. The families started to show up, the townspeople gathered, everyone wanted to know what happened, and most importantly, wanted to know what the Elder was going to do to retrieve the kidnapped women. The families were hysterical, angry even, and in need of a quick plan. Instead of looking to the chiefs of their respected villages, the people looked to the Elder for the answers. Hours had passed and the Elder hadn't come out of her hut to address the people. Instead, she sat smoking her cigar, staring off into space.

Elder, Asana whispered, how can I help? What would you like me to do? The Elder responded, "revenge my death; this is the work of the honeybee."

Elder? Asana responded, "but, you're not dead, you're still here, I'm still here, why would I need to revenge your death?" By all means, Asana, when you establish your own house, understand that that place is your Queendom. Do not allow anyone permission to destroy what you've built without fighting for it. If they enter your Queendom without respect, you have reason to be wrathful with a just cause. If they plan to disrupt your family, cut them off at the pass, and if they threaten the sanctity of your home, you are allowed to abandon your identity as a woman and dive deep into tradition to regain control. My Queendom has been destroyed, my reputation decimated, and two young girls have been ripped right from my bosom. I will return them to their families by morning, but I will die soon after."

"Elder, what would you like me to tell the people?" Asana, with a concerned look in her eyes, asked the Elder. "How should I tell them your plans Elder?"

Asana, your last lesson is this, The honeybee, the goat, the penguin, the boar and the whale. To love is war; no one escapes the torture of a controlling lover unless he understands that the lover will always become the enemy, and anyone standing in front of the beloved is prey. You must learn his character to survive this so-called love thing. It is fleeting & dangerous. At some point, the once-beloved becomes the hated, and the most enthralled of romances end in tragedy. The bitterness is all that remains when betrayal enters the room. Not a trace of love nor romance can be found. This is human nature. If you have to choose your poison, choose wisely.

The Goat: The buck in spirit is kindhearted. He's gentle with his affection but will not like your independence. As long as you oblige, he'll shower you with love. However, be aware that he will revenge if your love is unrequited or if he has to share your love with someone else, even his own children. He's fierce and will stop at nothing for reciprocal treatment, time, affection and care. He wants to be the only one.

The Penguin: The Cock will be faithful for life but will need control over the courtship, the house and the wealth. If you can relax and give him control, you'll find a great safe heaven with him. You can always trust his words, you can also trust his actions, just never appear wiser than him.

The Whale: The Bull is highly sexual and will require you to exhaust yourself in his pleasure. He will for sure take care of you but can be aggressive if he is sexually frustrated. He's the kind of man that will get bored easily and is looking for the next encounter. Never take him to be in love. He simply enjoys mating for as long as it's fun. He will however, be honest in his dealings, be sure to pay attention, and never cleave.

The Boar: The boar will allow a free thinker, he encourages independence, he is the only personality trait for a woman like you, Asana. He will protect you if necessary but will give you space enough to fly. The Boar is usually a male of great independence, assertiveness and bravery. He's a logical thinker, a mover and a shaker. He's confident but loving. He's hard to find because he is rarely in groups and generally likes to travel alone. To find him, you must walk into him by chance. You must be aligned in spirit, your heart must be pure and clean, and ready to further evolve as he's extremely intuitive. He's the man of the Gods; he's a blessing. To attract an encounter with him, you have to be a complete you. He will not accept mediocrity, nor a hateful woman. His only trouble is, he can easily walk away from a lover without regret or sorrow.

The Honeybee: A man without repentance, he's more sinister than anyone of the others. He has no intention of loving anyone other than himself. He mates with a fierce vengeance and is capable of engaging multiple women with no remorse. He's not fit for marriage, but many women fall victim to his charm, wit and presentation. He's packaged very well. Flashy and overconfident, this personality trait is what makes him dangerous; for women seeking something pure, he's the master of facades. He's the most dangerous because he will lie, steal and possibly kill for a woman he wants, knowing full well, his intentions are to serve him. He's self-serving and It's all a game of power. This is the selfishness of the Honeybee; he has the power to evoke in any woman the spirit of rage.

Today Asana, I am in Rage.

Rage

"Their rage supplies them with weapons." - Virgil "To control anger before it turns into rage is pure self-mastery."

K. McGhee

The Queendom has given us so many jewels and so much to unpack; I think it's best to start with how it ended. In Rage. The Elder's Rage could be seen as justifiable based on the events that transpired. Even the Elder's own teachings had not prepared Asana for what was to happen next.

What happened next will be covered in book 3. However, in regards to the rage, I want us to look into the emotion, feeling or otherwise expression of frustration known as rage. It's important for women to understand how rage works especially because some of the world's most diabolical crimes have come from lovers who have experienced moments of rage, plus it's important in obtaining Asana-hood. At such point, the woman is not only able to control such emotions, but is able to identify them before they erupt, channel them and act in a manner most sensible.

Let's dive deep. According to www.angermanage ment .co.uk, the general definition of rage is "the emotional expression of frustration centered on an inability to cope with negative thoughts, feelings, and external influences. Anger and rage are very different. Anger can manifest in a healthy and unhealthy way. Rage however, is an explosion of emotion that is out of control." As they further explain on their website, rage has no restrictions.

As we will learn later on in this chapter, there are different levels of rage and many different circumstances can throw an otherwise normal person into a bout of rage in an instant.

Many years ago, my mother had told me the story of a mother's rage. She went on to say a mother's rage is unmatched. There's no other rage on the planet quite like it. It wasn't until I was age forty-two that I began to understand what she meant. I was also able to identify several different forms of rage by this time. Most of the rage that I had witnessed in my lifetime had been linked to family, relationships, or fear. I've seen the most mild-mannered person pull a gun out on a person for breaking up with them. I've seen another thrown down the stairs, a person's property destroyed because of a failed marriage, a man's car burned because he ended a relationship, a new girlfriend beaten up because of jealousy, a fire started because of betrayal, the murder of a young woman and her husband's suicide because he feared losing her.

Here's the most interesting thing about rage, it can happen to any person, anytime, anywhere. No one's off-limits. My mentor, Baaba Heru of the Studio of Ptah says that within each of us is the making of a gangster, a murderer, or thief, but it is the cultivation of our personality that moves us further from this truth. Generally speaking, most rage is an accumulation of unresolved issues that are linked to moments of anger. However, there can be some mental health issues attached to recurrent bouts of rage. According to Harvard Medicine Magazine, depression and anger go hand and hand.

What the elder was feeling was a calculated, planned, calm revenge, this is the worst kind of rage and it is what would have been known to my mother as a mother's rage. What the Prince had done to Elder Eden and the kidnapping was the act of the Honeybee fluttering his wings in violence because he couldn't have things his way. The Elder stood in the way of him reaching Asana, and thus his rage was an act of terrorism. Be aware of rage, not just your own, but also the possible bouts from other people. It could lead to destruction.

Delayed Gratification

If the Elder was speaking, she would tell you, "beloved do not go falling in love with any old soul." She would tell you to be mindful of the impact that falling could have on your body and how holding in bitterness could wrinkle your skin and age your womb. She would tell you to read the personality type of your mate and decide if your target is a useful lover worth entertaining. She would say without a doubt that in love, delayed gratification is a wise woman's secret weapon to attraction, allure and romance.

Learn how to slow down and take your time. Especially in love or dating. If you can apply this method to business and creative ventures, you'll find that success falls not too far behind your well thought out actions. Allow moments of evaluation and consideration; you'll find that delayed gratification will challenge how far you are willing to go to develop a strong body and a strong mind by way of denying your flesh of immediate gratification. Mastering the art of waiting will also help with impulsive responses or behaviors which often lead to regret. The idea that getting what you want when you want it as you want it seems like the ideal life. However, I believe it's a loftier side of the reality because the truth is, oftentimes what we want are based on our surface-level understanding. It never has depth, and often we regret wanting something so bad to only find out that what we wanted really was not what we anticipated it to be. This includes lovers, jobs, things etc. However, on the flip side, it's the desires that are carved out and that are intentional and aligned that we find more pleasure and enjoyment. To master the art of "intentional action "is delayed gratification in action. It's the ability to wait for a larger reward. The payoff is considered before the action. The question of what's in it for me moves the thought to a desire.

If you can become okay with contemplation, you'll find much more things in life to enjoy simply by paying attention to your desires and understanding why you desire them to begin with. Allow yourself some time to sit with your desires. Don't be afraid to want something or someone without seeing immediate results. Allow your self-time to put it out into the atmosphere so that thing you want comes to you.

Take the time to want, and while waiting, craving and desiring that thing you want, align yourself with your desires by visualizing that thing as you want it. Begin to see it, feel it, taste it, dream it and carve it out. You'll find that the longer you sit with your desires, the greater the experience once you've decided to engage. The longer you sit patiently with your desires wanting them, the more energy builds and instead of chasing that thing, the universe picks up the vibrations and sends them to you. Often, we mess up divine creation because we get in the way. The universe has a way of packaging things to our liking and for our good. It also can weed out the wrongs and sending things as they should be for our spiritual and personal development. When we get in the way of things trying to control the outcome, trying to move things faster, we are often left unfulfilled. Asana-hood is learning how to co-create with the world around us, by using the energy in the world within us. We must not chase. We must allow. We must become comfortable with slowing down and taking time.

We can use this theory in not just love and business, but also in friendships and all other matters of living. To act in haste or to be hotheaded are not in line with femininity and attracting the life you want. Now not acting in haste, or waiting, or mastering the art of delayed gratification, does not equate to non-action, but it's the kind that moves your desires closer to you. The work on your part is to keep your desires high, but your vibrations are even higher. While waiting, keep loving, keep living, keep believing and mastering yourself along this journey. Do not be sidetracked by your desires; let them be, and soon enough, you'll see that the very thing you wanted has come to you. Enjoy your moments and find joy in the happenings of everyday living and loving; when you are light, it's hard for the things you want to elude you.

In love and relationships, be wise to delay the act of Queendom building with a proposed mate until you can identify your lover's personality type. Decide if you are compatible based on both of your personality types and needs and allow things to unfold organically. To delay the act of becoming emotionally attached before you have identified your lover's needs and what you want from your lover will make for a much sweeter love.

Moving In Unison

Moving in unison is essential to healthy relationships, but before you've entered a relationship, you must move inward. Align with self, align with your desires and plan them out in your head, feel them and allow the universe to move on your behalf. You'll know it's right by how natural and organic it feels. Understand that your ideal mate is somewhere out there, moving closer and closer to you. Through the either he's making his way forward. Your job is to move in unison. It's important that you learn that attraction is happening as you move about, as you go about your daily life. As you are engaging and moving about, your possible lover is always watching. Be sure to give a show.

The language of the human body is not only a universal language, but it can be a subconscious ethereal way to evoke emotions in others, change behaviors and communicate one's intentions.

What's quite common to many is the fact that most people are aware of the concept of body language, but most have never explored the idea of understanding how it works and how to use it for themselves. The deeper transcendental idea of a universal sacred body movements science system can help many learn how to communicate non-verbally, but spiritually.

Sacred body movements & energy preservation is key when dealing with femininity. From voice and inflection and tone, from slowly annunciating to only speaking when necessary all of these things are but examples of controlling one's body and being in tune with one's energy emission.

To control the energy in your own body gives you a power that will allow you to impact atmospheres and environments much like the Elder when she walks down a street. Much of what you are about to learn in this chapter will take years of commitment and dedication, as you evolve as a woman, you'll become much more aware of your body and will become much more aligned.

To improve your feminine powers is to become aware of how you move your body when you are communicating. You must become aware of every move and do so with intent, the sway of your hips when you walk, to the pulsating pout of your lips, the slight tilt in your head when you nod in agreement, to the movement of your hands when you speak. Once you understand that every movement has the power to cause movement/motion and evoke emotion in your environment and in those in your, environment you'll become much more in control of everything that moves about your environment.

It's equally important to be aware of your posture when you're not moving about. Great posture is head of the table when we are speaking about universal body language or when we are talking about moving in unison with all around you. Your posture sends sub minimal messages about your confidence levels, it also teaches people just how well established and how self-aware you are. This silent message will have people either respect you at the onset of meeting you or approaching you from the level into which your posture resembles. A depressed man will attract an opportunist, pull those shoulders up, relax that back and be mindful of your posture.

Here are five ways to improve your posture.

1. Be sure to not lean forward when walking or sitting.
2. Strengthen your core muscles. Core exercises can help with poor posture.
3. A posture corrector back brace is helpful to wear for sometime; wear a few times a week to help.
4. Practicing Yoga is a great way to improve your posture.
5. Be sure that you have a fitting and comfortable underwear.

Considering being aware of your body movements while communicating, it's important to note that once your hips have attracted your person of interest, every moment thereafter needs to speak honestly to your interest. Move less, more slowly and more deliberately. Try to keep your hands in view, generally in front of you or near your lap. The hands are a very seductive tool; use them. Try not to hide them or overuse them by playing on electronic devices, your cell phones or obsessively moving about. Keeping them in sight shows the person you're communicating with that you are indeed engaged. Use them as settle reminders of how feminine you are. Your well-manicured nails will always be a point of interest for the masculine. Your extremely soft hands will speak to your self-care methods and can send signals that you are a soft and gentle woman. This communicating with another is all silent. All subliminal, all effective and most alluring.

Engage and use your silent communication skills

Here are 5 ways to use body language to communicate

1. Be sure that your audience is engaged and is ready to consume what you have to share.
2. Be aware of your topic and speak at eye level, so if the person is sitting, you follow suit. If they are standing, you do the same; make sure you are eye level when speaking.
3. Be sure to be as close to the person as they are comfortable with, pay attention to cues that signal you might be too close. A slight nudge, a gentle touch of the hand can be off-putting if you are not paying attention. If you can clearly see they are comfortable, it's okay to remove an out of place hair, swat a bug off of a jacket trim, or even better if necessary, hold hands when trying to make an emotional statement.
4. Listen intently. Be sure that you listen not just with your ears but also with your eyes, be sure to be pay attention and be totally involved in what the person is saying.
5. Repeat - and call their name. Once you notice a point of interest in something the person has said, repeat it back to them, offer your input and call them by name.

The Connection

There is nothing unclear about equal interest. You'll never be confused about a potential love interest. Energetically lovers destined to encounter one another as the universe would have it would equally want to experience the other. If you've met a mate that you are extremely in love with, but the love is unrequited, perhaps you're not a vibrational match at this time. Now that does not mean that you will never be; it just means it should not be - right now. There are those strange times when one lover is ahead of the other vibrationally, but please note, there is nothing you can do about being unmatched. Nothing, no amount of convincing, beautifying yourself, nothing. The only thing you can do is to vibrate higher and allow the universe to organize your divine connection.

A lot of lovers are heartbroken coming to this conclusion because oftentimes, they've already invested so much in the other person that they feel entitled to the love in return, but that's not how love works, nor divine connection. When a divine connection is present, the light from one will illuminate the other and vice versa. There is no confusion; there is no need to think about what it is because it just is. Here's some hard truth for many people. Divine connection does not equate to forever. In some cases, the connection is used as a catalyst for something greater than the two; other times, the connection was designed for a short while, and for the extremely aligned destinies of the two are intertwined. Either way, divine connection is a gift and beauty is always the result.

About The Author

Twenty plus years in the field of Alternative Medicine, Karema McGhee is a Complementary Alternative Medicine practitioner from New Jersey, now residing in North Carolina. Over the past 20 years, she's operated an online Holistic Health school and 2 Holistic Wellness Centers. Her passion over the last 20 years has been her health freedom advocacy work, teaching as many people the art of whole-body wellness.

Leading her practice with the idea that for every illness there is a cure, and the idea that integrated medicine is necessary more now than ever. Her primary alternative medicine modality is herbal medicine, both Eastern & Western, with Indian influence.

May your heart be loved, and your soul be satisfied for good.

Asana Energy

30 Day Transformation Journal

This journal is a personal commitment to your feminine development.

A woman on a quest for refinement, selfdevelopment and feminine power must first look within.

There are two important things to remember over the next thirty days.

1. No one else is responsible for your happiness. Over the next thirty days your energy will be focused on creating the happiness you seek.
2. We cannot become Asana or experience our Asana energy until we refine the hardest and toughest places of ourselves. You will write and take note of your journey for thirty days attempting to soften those places.

Day 1

ARE YOU ASANA OR THE BEGGAR?

Day 2

WHAT DO YOU WANT TO MANIFEST IN THE NEXT 30 DAYS?

Day 3

WHAT IS IT ABOUT YOUR LIFE THAT BRINGS YOU JOY?

Day 4

WHAT WILL MAKE YOU HAPPY?

_____
_____
_____
_____
_____
_____
_____
_____
_____
_____
_____
_____
_____
_____
_____

Day 5

ARE YOU HAPPY?

Day 6

ARE YOU AFRAID?

HOW CONFIDENT ARE YOU?

Day 8

LET'S DO A 48 HOUR UNPLUG FROM SOCIAL MEDIA. HOW DO YOU FEEL ABOUT THAT?

Day 9

HOW DO YOU FEEL RIGHT NOW?

Day 10

ARE YOU READY TO CHANGE YOUR LIFE?

Day 11

WHAT WAS YOUR BEST RELATIONSHIP AND WHY?

Day 12

WHAT BRINGS YOU PEACE OF MIND?

Day 13

DO YOU HAVE ANY PAST HURT?

Day 14

HOW CAN YOU IMPROVE YOUR LIFE?

Day 15

WHAT ARE YOUR TALENTS, WHAT MAKES YOU DIFFERENT?

_____
_____
_____
_____
_____
_____
_____
_____
_____
_____
_____

Day 16

ARE YOU COMMITTED TO YOUR EVOLUTION?

Day 17

WHO ARE YOU?

Day 18

YOU HAVE A RIGHT TO RE-INVENT YOURSELF AS MANY TIMES AS YOU LIKE, IS IT TIME?

Day 19

WHAT CAN YOU DO
TO IMPROVE YOUR SELF-ESTEEM?

Day 20

IT'S A GOOD IDEA TO START DOING THINGS FOR YOUR PERSONAL HEALING, WHAT'S NEXT?

Day 21

LET'S CONSIDER GETTING FIT.
TIME TO CONTACT A FITNESS TRAINER.

Day 22

IT MIGHT BE TIME TO CONSIDER A DIET AND NUTRITION SPECIALIST, LET'S GET THAT DONE.

Day 23

HAVE YOU CONSIDERED A THERAPIST?

Day 24

IT'S TIME TO LEARN A NEW SKILL, LANGUAGE OR SPORT. TIME TO CONTACT THE RIGHT PEOPLE TO MAKE IT HAPPEN.

Day 25

IT' MIGHT BE TIME FOR A NEW HAIR STYLE, COLOR OR LENGTH. CONSIDER CHANGING IT UP.

Day 26

TIME TO CLEAN OUT YOUR CLOSETS. TIME FOR A NEW WARDROBE, SOFTER FABRICS, BRIGHTER COLORS

Day 27

TIME TO FIND A SIGNATURE FRAGRANCE. PERHAPS NOT A FRAGRANCE EVERYONE IS WEARING, BUT ONE THAT IS UNIQUE TO YOU.

Day 28

TIME TO CONSIDER IF A MOVE IS NECESSARY. DOES YOUR ENVIRONMENT INSPIRE YOU?

Day 29

TIME TO CONSIDER YOUR FRIENDS. ARE THEY SUPPORTIVE, OR REMOTELY CLOSE TO THE WOMAN YOU ARE LOOKING TO BECOME?

Day 30

TIME TO DELETE THOSE OLD TEXT MESSAGES, SCREENSHOTS & PHONE NUMBERS OF ANYONE NOT ALIGNED WITH YOUR PERSONAL & SPIRITUAL GOALS.

www.ingramcontent.com/pod-product-compliance
Lightning Source LLC
Chambersburg PA
CBHW071350080526
44587CB00017B/3042